Queen Mary 2
BOOK OF COMPARISONS

Conceived and designed by
The Open Agency
Mill House
8 Mill Street
London SE1 2BA
www.openagency.com

Commissioned illustrations by **Andrew Davidson**

Written by **Elspeth Wills**

First published 2003
© The Open Agency Limited
Commissioned illustrations © Andrew Davidson 2003

ISBN 0-9542451-3-X

Printed in China.

CONTENTS

THE pictures shown in this booklet are designed to convey a practical noti of the immense size of the Cunard leviathan steamers "LUSITANI and "MAURETANIA." These vessels are the fastest in the world, a their dimensions are:—

Length	... ...	790 feet.	
Breadth	... ...	88 ,,	
Depth to Boat Deck	... ...	80 ,,	
Draught (fully loaded)	... ...	37 ft. 6 in.	
Displacement on load draught	... ...	45,000 tons.	
Horse-Power of Turbine Engines	... ...	68,000	
Height to tops of Funnels	... ...	155 feet.	
Height to Mastheads	... ...	216 ,,	
Passenger accommodation	...	1st Class 500.	
,, ,,	... ...	2nd ,, 500.	
,, ,,	... ...	3rd ,, 1,300.	
Crew	.. ..	... 800 to 900.	

The exact meaning of these dimensions will perhaps be more clearly realised the illustrations. The contrasts are drawn to scale, and show in pictorial form some the most imposing examples of architectural and engineering skill, side by side with o or other of the ships. Their huge size is, after all, but the least remarkable feature of the mammoth Cunarders. Each is propelled by four screws rotated by turbine engines 68,000 horse-power. In other words, this is the measure of the work done by the engin of one of these vessels. Sixty-eight thousand horses placed head to tail in a single li would extend 90 miles, as far as from London to the Isle of Wight, while, if the stee were harnessed twenty abreast, there would be no fewer than 3,400 rows of power horses. The passenger accommodation of these ships is no less wonderful. magnificence and comfort is unsurpassed by any other vessel, while the great size a height of the public saloons and private staterooms, combined with their exquisite desi and sumptuous decorations and appointments, make it almost impossible to realise th

THE TRADITION CONTINUES

'Colossus . . . Leviathan . . . Queen of the Ocean . . . Grand Hotel at Sea'. For over a century Cunard liners have inspired superlatives to convey their size, elegance and style.

Queen Mary 2 proudly follows in the wake of her illustrious predecessors as one of the seven wonders of the ocean. The first liner to be built in the new millennium, she measures up to the world's great buildings in scale and matches global symbols of travel in performance. The public have always had a love affair with liners. Posters, postcards, commemorative books and cigarette cards were produced in ever increasing volumes to captivate their imagination and satisfy their hunger for information. Figures helped people to grasp the sheer size, power and engineering of these 'wonder ships'. The Lusitania was longer than the frontage of the world's largest cathedral: the Queen Mary was taller than the Niagara Falls. Horsepower, ice cream consumption, the number of light bulbs, there seemed to be no limit to the comparisons drawn.

'Queen Mary 2 Book of Comparisons' honours a tradition started in 1907 to celebrate the maiden voyages of the Mauretania and Lusitania and continued in 1936 for the first Queen Mary. As the story of QM2 unfolds, the unique illustrations commissioned for this book draw new analogies, from the whales of the deep to the spinning planets of the heavens, which still set the imagination racing.

Above Cover of *'The Queen Mary - A Book of Comparisons'* (1936).
Left Introduction from *'Lusitania and Mauretania - Cunard Express Turbine Steamers: Some Interesting Comparisons'* (1907).

RULER OF THE OCEAN

Queen Mary 2 is quite simply the longest passenger vessel ever built.

On land people have always reached for the sky since the Egyptians first built pyramids to honour their rulers. Four millennia later, the spire of the 850 foot Transamerica Pyramid in San Francisco now punctures the clouds. On the ocean, for centuries people have built ever longer ships to conquer the crests of the wild Atlantic waves.

At 1,132 feet Queen Mary 2 is longer than the Eiffel Tower is tall. She could stretch the length of four blocks of Fifth Avenue and like the Queen Mary before her, she measures up to the world's tallest hotel on land – the Burj al Arab in Dubai.

She towers above the 23 storey building on Broadway from which Cunard once directed the American operations of the largest passenger shipping line in the world. QM2 is the flagship of Cunard Line, part of Carnival Corporation, the world's largest cruise ship owner.

Above In the 1930s the Queen Mary measured up to the world's great landmarks. Seventy years later QM2 challenges a new world skyline.

Britannia 230ft (70m) Date 1840

St Paul's Cathedral (London) 365ft (111m) Date 1710

Swiss Re Building (London) 590ft (180m) Date 2004

Chrysler Building (New York) 1046ft (319m) Date 1930

Burj al Arab (Dubai) 1053ft (321m) Date 1999

Queen Mary 1019ft (311m) Date 1936

Bank of China (Hong Kong) 1209ft (369m) Date 1990

Queen Mary 2 1132ft (345m) Date 2004

Transamerica Pyramid (San Francisco) 853ft (260m) Date 1972

Eiffel Tower (Paris) 986ft (300m) Date 1889

Cunard Building (New York) 361ft (110m) Date 1921

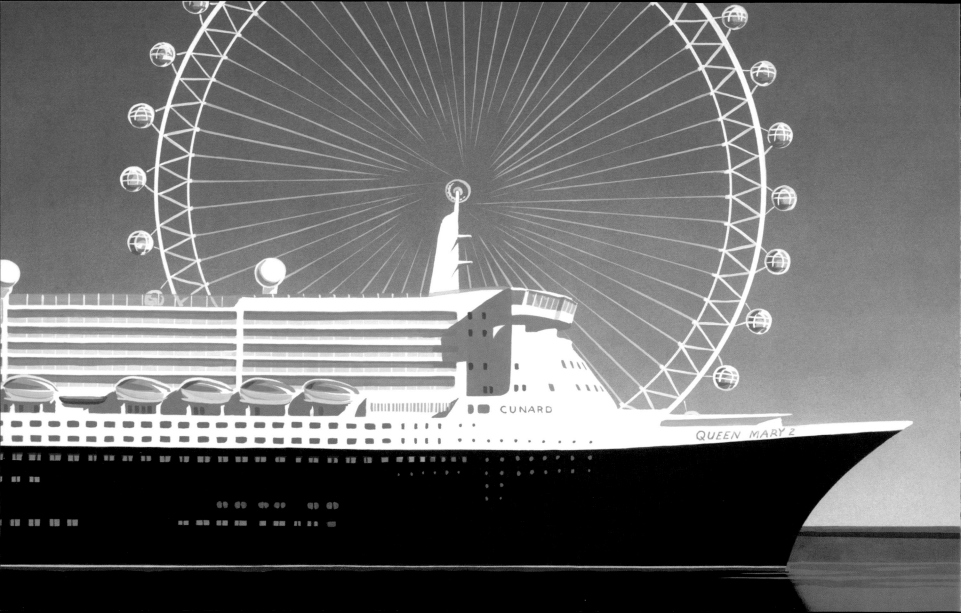

SAILING TALL

Queen Mary 2 is the tallest passenger vessel ever built, rising 237 feet from the base of her keel to the top of her proud funnel. She is half as high as the London Eye, the tallest observation wheel in the world.

These two iconic structures share remarkable parallels of audacity and imagination. Both were conceived to celebrate human achievement as the new millennium dawned. Each is a hugely complex structure, testing technology to its limits in the quest to balance performance and safety. Yet these giants are both dependent on the tide in their very different ways.

The parts that make up the London Eye had to be small enough to be floated upstream under London's many bridges while Queen Mary 2 has to be low enough to sail under New York's Verrazano-Narrows Bridge which she clears by only ten feet. When the Queen Mary was launched, people compared her with Tower Bridge, the structure that for most people symbolised London. Now the world's tallest passenger vessel, a foot higher than Tower Bridge, and the capital's newest landmark look each other in the eye.

Above The pinnacles of Tower Bridge were two feet higher than the Queen Mary, measured from the base of her keel to the tip of her masthead.

A SEVENTEEN DECKER QUEEN

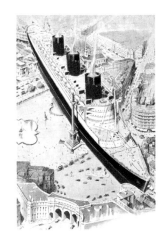

As well as being the longest passenger vessel on the ocean, Queen Mary 2 is also the widest in the world. The combined area of the Queen Mary and QM2 would entirely fill Trafalgar Square.

While the Queen Mary carried two red double deckers on her final passage in 1967 so that passengers could claim to have travelled round Cape Horn on top of a London bus, QM2 could accommodate a fleet of six hundred London buses within her 3.5 acre footprint.

The seventeen decks of QM2 tower over Nelson's Column whose base is guarded by four ceremonial lions. They acknowledge their elder, the golden lion rampant of Cunard, a symbol of maritime prestige for over 160 years. Cunarders and London buses, icons of travel on land and sea, both wear distinctive liveries. Samuel Cunard chose red and black for the funnels of his first fleet in 1840, almost 70 years before the fleet of red London buses took to the streets.

Above QM2 is 113 feet longer than the Queen Mary which could comfortably slice Trafalgar Square in two.

GIANTS OF THE DEEP

The hull alone of Queen Mary 2 is 50,000 tons, more than the total weight of a school of 330 blue whales.

The blue whale, the largest animal ever to inhabit the Earth, would recognise a kindred spirit in QM2. Both have rounded 'noses' and streamlined bodies to reduce resistance as they move through the water. Each communicates with fellow voyagers, and steers its passage over hundreds of miles, the whales by sound and sonar, QM2 by radio and radar. Reverberations from the voice of the blue whale, the loudest animal on Earth, and from a blast on QM2's whistle can both be felt up to a hundred miles away.

The whale's front flippers help it to balance its immense body while QM2's four 166 square foot folding fins keep her stable in the wildest seas. She is a purebred ocean liner, the first to be built for almost 40 years. The thick steel plates of her hull, the power of her engines, the rake of her prow and her lean, ocean greyhound lines allow her to punch through the towering waves in an Atlantic gale. She ventures where no cruise ship dares. The speed of QM2 on an Atlantic crossing leaves cruise ships and blue whales standing as she forges ahead at a maximum speed of over 30 knots in a direct line for her destination. She travels well in excess of the speed and range of a Caribbean cruise ship and twice as fast as the average speed of her fellow giant of the deep.

Above The Queen Mary was a weighty lady. Her rudder alone was 140 tons and her two bow anchors each weighed 16 tons.

A MIGHTY LADY

The longest, the tallest and the widest passenger vessel, Queen Mary 2 is also the largest ever built. She is nearly twice as large as the Queen Mary and three times the size of the legendary Titanic. She could carry a fleet of 130 Britannias within her immense hold.

Gross tonnage is the internationally recognised measure of size on the ocean, as the second is to time or the knot to speed at sea. It expresses the internal volume of a ship rather than its weight. On this count QM2 achieves a staggering 150,000 gross tons.

The history of tonnage stretches back to 13th century England where a ton or 'tun' was a wine barrel with a capacity of 252 gallons. When Parliament sought to tax imported wine, it based the duty on how many tuns a ship could carry, fixing the weight of the full barrel at 2,240 pounds and the space that it occupied at approximately 42 cubic feet. Over time gross tonnage came to reflect the overall carrying capacity of a ship.

Gross tonnage is a vessel's defining characteristic and at the time Samuel Cunard was rightly proud of his 1,135 ton Britannia, the 'plain but comfortable boat' that became the first regular passenger steamer to ply the Atlantic.

Above This Churchman's cigarette card is one of a series of 50 produced to celebrate the Queen Mary's maiden voyage. It illustrated the fact that the Queen Mary's tonnage was 63 times that of the Britannia. QM2 more than doubles that figure again.

Britannia (1840 - 1849) gross tonnage 1,135

Scotia (1862 - 1904) gross tonnage 3,871

Etruria (1885 - 1910) gross tonnage 7,718

Saxonia (1900 - 1925) gross tonnage 14,281

Aquitania (1914 - 1949) gross tonnage 45,647

Queen Mary (1936 - 1967) gross tonnage 80,774

Queen Mary 2 (2004 -) gross tonnage 150,000

BLOCK 850

The 185 ton Block 850 is the bridge of Queen Mary 2, one of the last pieces of a giant jigsaw to be swung into place. While the world's largest jigsaw has 45,000 pieces, the hull alone of Queen Mary 2 is made up of six times that number.

Some of her 300,000 pieces are measured in inches and weigh pounds: others may be 35 yards long and weigh 400 tons. They have been fitted together into 580 panels and 94 blocks. From the bridge to the ballroom hundreds of other pieces and panels create her superstructure.

Building QM2 began with a naval architect's vision and its translation from paper to steel. It took a million man hours to design QM2 and eight million such hours to build her: 80,000 individual plans were drawn to ensure that every piece would fit. When a 15 foot scale model, accurate in every detail was tested, QM2 was declared seaworthy even when buffeted by a hurricane in her simulation tank. The Queen Mary Project became job no. G32 on 6th November, 2000 when the contract was signed between Cunard Line and ALSTOM Chantiers de l'Atlantique, Europe's largest shipyard. Twenty months later, on the order of Cunard Line's Master, a giant overhead crane swung block number 502 into place. This was the first piece of the puzzle, the 600 ton keel which, in a time honoured maritime tradition, had two coins welded on to it for good fortune.

Above The first Queen Mary used very different shipbuilding techniques. Her hull was made up of giant steel plates riveted together by swarms of shipyard workers clambering like ants over her scaffolding.

A BILLION SPARKS OF FIRE

Over nine hundred miles of welding fuse the thousands of elements of Queen Mary 2 into a liner. It is enough to weld together again both sides of the land which opened up forty million years ago to form the English Channel.

Since the Servia was launched in 1881, the hulls of Cunarders have been built of steel, one of the world's toughest metals. Steel underpins many global engineering icons from the Eiffel Tower and the Forth Bridge to the London Eye and QM2.

At the St Nazaire shipyard on France's Atlantic seaboard, 1,500 metal workers shaped and welded thousands of tons of steel, every piece chalked with its G32 job number. In the two panel fabrication lines, each one as long as five football pitches, panels, made from these pieces, were fitted with the appropriate components from portholes to the pipework that weaves its 310 mile way through the ship. Special vehicles whose twelve pairs of tyres can resist the pressure of a 270 ton load pulled the panels to the pre-assembly zone where they were welded together into blocks. Two giant cranes then swung the blocks into place as QM2 rose ever upwards and outwards in her dry dock.

On 21st March, 2003 the dock was flooded, the gates opened and a new liner greeted the Atlantic. Nine months later, QM2 made her first crossing of the English Channel to reach her home port of Southampton.

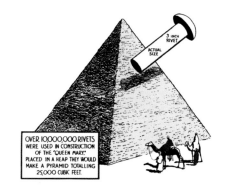

OVER 10,000,000 RIVETS WERE USED IN CONSTRUCTION OF THE "QUEEN MARY." PLACED IN A HEAP THEY WOULD MAKE A PYRAMID TOTALLING 25,000 CUBIC FEET.

Above Over ten million rivets were used in building the Queen Mary. Her architect described them as 'the human fingerprints of a great ship'.

CROWNING GLORY

Four of the mighty Eurostar locomotives that speed through the Channel Tunnel would fit into Queen Mary 2's funnel, 44 feet by 22 feet at its widest point.

The final third of her funnel had to be added once she was afloat as the gantry crane bridging the dock's entrance lacked the headroom for a crowned queen. From funnel to fore deck, QM2's design picks up echoes from the past. Her bow was inspired by the Normandie (1935), the Queen Mary's rival which was built by the same St Nazaire shipyard as QM2. Some public spaces on QM2 also draw on the Art Deco style epitomised by these two great liners.

Her funnel is modelled on that of QE2 which caused a sensation when first revealed to the public because of its modernistic lines and revolutionary wind scoop at the base. As the vessel moves forward, air is channelled up the scoop which pushes the exhaust fumes up and away from the decks, freeing space for sunbathing and deck sports.

Wearing its traditional livery of 'Cunard Red' and black, QM2's funnel carries the proud voice of the ship. She has four whistles, one of which was previously carried on the Queen Mary's middle funnel throughout her thirty year career. As she sails through the Straits of Gibraltar the tone of QM2's deep bass A could be heard on two Continents, Africa and Europe.

Above Three express locomotives could line up inside one of the Queen Mary's three massive funnels.

ROLLS ROYCE OF THE OCEAN

Queen Mary 2 is one of the largest manmade objects ever built that moves under its own power. Her engines produce the thrust to launch a Boeing 747 or to maintain three cruising at 530 miles per hour.

Her 170,000 horsepower engines are the work horses of the ship. The power of aircraft and liners, however technologically advanced, has been measured in horsepower since James Watt patented his steam engine in 1769. The work done by QM2's engines is equivalent to that of a line of horses stretching the 235 miles from Halifax, Nova Scotia, birthplace of Samuel Cunard, to Boston where his first transatlantic paddle steamer arrived in 1840.

QM2 is the first vessel to be escorted by four Mermaids. Her engines drive four Rolls Royce/ALSTOM Mermaid propeller pods which extend beneath her hull. The pods, each weighing more than 250 tons, are the largest and most powerful ever made. The two forward pods are fixed and the two aft pods are steerable allowing the largest passenger vessel in the world to turn full circle. A touch on a button on the pilot's chair controls all QM2's manoeuvres whereas it took four men to hold down the first Cunarder's wheel in a storm.

Above From pony to racing thoroughbred - when the 66,000 hp Lusitania was launched in 1906, Cunard compared the might of her turbine-powered engines with that of her predecessors. The engines of QM2 generate over two hundred times more horsepower than the steam engines that paddled the plucky Britannia across the Atlantic.

THE SOUL OF A LINER

The 20,000 workers involved in the creation of Queen Mary 2 could line her decks in celebration of the ship which they built.

In doing so they would beat the record held to this day by the Queen Mary which once transported over 16,000 troops across the Atlantic on a single voyage at the height of the Second World War.

Since antiquity sailors have believed that their ships have a soul and a life of their own. From the ship owner who dreamed of a great ocean liner to the worker who made the last weld, many thousands of people have dedicated their lives to create the soul of QM2. Artists, book-keepers, crane drivers, draughtsmen, electricians, fitters, glaziers, hydrologists, installers, joiners, kitchen designers, labourers, metallurgists, naval architects, oceanographers, painters, quality controllers, riggers, surveyors, telecoms engineers, underwriters, ventilation experts and welders - there are too many to name. In the 37 months from signing the contract to delivering the vessel, St Nazaire has been home to people from all over the world.

Scots were among the many nationalities who helped to build QM2 exporting the same shipbuilding tradition which led Cunard to order most of its ships on the Clyde, from the Britannia to the first three Queens. In 1861 John Scott, a Clyde shipbuilder who had worked on vessels for Samuel Cunard, was invited to France to set up the St Nazaire shipyard from which the Normandie, the France and QM2 were launched, all legends in their lifetime.

Above Crewing a liner at sea requires a different army of skills. From the orchestra to the black squad who fed the boilers, the ranks of the Mauretania numbered 1,800.

LIGHT TO PORT

Capable of providing electricity for half of the city which was Cunard Line's original home port, Queen Mary 2 could light up the skyline of Liverpool's waterfront.

Two gas turbines and four diesel engines are the powerhouse of a town at sea. Over two thirds of the energy generated goes towards driving QM2's pod propellers which move her across the ocean. The other third meets onboard needs from lighting passenger cabins to powering the computers and instruments that help make QM2 the most technologically advanced passenger vessel of all time.

For half a century lights burned until midnight on Liverpool's waterfront not only when a Cunarder was in port but when the blueprint for a new liner was being debated within the shipping line's headquarters. Sandwiched between the early skyscraper of the Royal Liver insurance headquarters and the Renaissance palace housing the port authority, the Cunard building became one of Liverpool's Three Graces.

Today, as Cunard's fourth Queen takes to the seas, a fourth Grace is rising on Liverpool's Pierhead. This stunning piece of architecture includes a museum telling the history of Cunard's first home port and honouring the nine million emigrants who, between 1830 and 1930, bade a last farewell to their old life as they boarded their ship for North America.

30,000 ELECTRIC LAMPS ILLUMINATE *The* "QUEEN MARY"

Above As once the glow from the 30,000 bulbs on the Queen Mary sparkled across the night ocean, satellites now track the 80,000 lights on QM2 from space.

RED CARPET TREATMENT

Caring for the 280,000 square yards of carpet on Queen Mary 2 is like hoovering the athletics stadium of the 2004 Olympic Games in Athens ten times over.

Ocean housekeeping includes beating the exotic rugs in the six deck high Grand Lobby and treating with respect the piece of carpet from the captain's dayroom of the Queen Mary, gifted to Captain Ronald Warwick, the first Master of QM2.

A red runner will be rolled out in August, 2004 when the liner berths at Piraeus for the Olympic Games, as she has been chartered by the Games Organising Committee to become a temporary floating hotel. Olympic athletes will pound her teak decks as they did on the Queen Mary before her. The most unusual ocean sprint was undertaken during her sea trials in 1936. Lord Burghley the British Olympic athlete, conducted his own speed trials in full evening dress by running a 400 yard lap around the Promenade Deck in under 60 seconds. Although athletes could run a 600 yard race along QM2's Promenade Deck most passengers prefer to stroll along it or view it from a steamer chair as they engage in the gentle socialising that has always been the hallmark of a liner crossing.

Above Scores of the 'latest improved vacuum cleaners' hoovered the Queen Mary's six miles of carpet.

STEP BY STEP

Ascending the 5,000 stairs on Queen Mary 2 is the equivalent of climbing a giant staircase carved in the rock of South Africa's 3,567 foot high Table Mountain.

Passengers on QM2 can follow in the footsteps of Marlene Dietrich on the original Queen Mary, making a regal entrance down the sweep of the branching Grand Staircase or pausing for effect on the grande descente to the Britannia restaurant. Deep within the hull of the ship the crew climb ladder rungs and descend in service elevators as they traverse the maze of passages that lead to wine cellars, baggage stores and galleys.

From the 1870s passengers savoured the novelty of travelling by elevator on the ocean and by the 1930s elevators were transporting baggage, laundry, kitchen supplies and cars as well as passengers, strictly divided by class. The crew had separate elevators: it would not be proper for a tuxedoed gentleman bound for champagne cocktails to travel with a greaser from the engine room. Although 21st century cruising is classless, five of QM2's two storey staterooms have private elevators and a butler on call.

Two panoramic elevators travel up the side of QM2, giving new meaning to a room with a sea view.

Above This model of the Queen Mary which fanned out to show individual deck plans not only made a memorable keepsake but also helped passengers to negotiate her 12 decks linked by a maze of stairs, corridors and elevators.

THE WORLD'S LONGEST WASHING LINE

The 17,000 sheets laundered on Queen Mary 2 during a transatlantic crossing would make up the Britannia's billowing sails a hundred times over.

The *'*QUEEN MARY*'*
*'*HOUSEHOLD*'*
EQUIPMENT

210,000 TOWELS
30,000 SHEETS
31,000 PILLOW CASES
AND THOUSANDS of
OTHER PIECES

21,000
TABLE CLOTHS

92,000
NAPKINS

Above The Queen Mary, which made 1001 Atlantic crossings over her 30 year lifetime, had a gargantuan appetite for laundry.

Although the Britannia steamed across the Atlantic in 1840, she carried a full set of sails in case her engines broke down in mid ocean. Crew on the Britannia knew their sheets from their ropes. When asked to trim the main sail, they pulled on the sheets, the ropes that controlled it. The 1,250 crew on QM2 speak a very different maritime language, although they too instinctively know their port from their starboard and chew the fat in their off duty hours.

The 89 strong crew of the Britannia would recognise some job titles within QM2's hierarchy - the steward, the surgeon, the baker and the Master of Arms. They might grasp the meaning of others - hotel manager, spa attendant, shop assistant - but never place them in the context of a ship. Over the centuries the Cunard barometer has risen from basic comfort to luxury although QM2's captain still obeys Samuel Cunard's instruction of 'safety before speed'.

THE GLOBE IN A CABIN

Through its unique interactive television system QM2 has the virtual equivalent of a bellboy in every cabin.

Passengers can order a brandy, view a video, arrange a session in the gym or book their next passage at the touch of a key. The steward who delivers the order is trained to the White Star standard: Cunard's legendary service remains a constant on the most technologically advanced passenger liner ever built.

Above 'Perhaps the single feature of the new "Queen Mary" which will most impress a passenger with her extreme modernity is the fact that he can pick up the telephone on the bedside table of his stateroom and talk with friends in New York, London, Paris . . . or any other part of the civilised world.'

When travelling to the 1936 Berlin Olympic Games on Cunard's Samaria, James Naismith, the inventor of basketball, wrote home to his wife in Kansas. His letter travelled over 5,000 miles and took nearly two weeks to reach her. Had he been sailing on QM2, his electronic postcard would travel 22,300 miles in a split second. Emails, telephone conversations and internet communications bounce off the Immarsat satellite high above the Equator which connects the world's lonely places, from Antarctica to the mid-Atlantic, beyond the reach of cellular or fixed communications.

Naismith kept in touch with the news of the impending Olympics by reading the Samaria's onboard newspaper while on the Queen Mary passengers followed the progress of the Games by radio, broadcast from 38 loudspeakers positioned throughout the ship. QM2's passengers watch the Olympics, play basketball or check the weather without having to leave their cabins.

FLYING THE FLAGSHIP

It would take five double-decker A380 Airbuses to transport the 2,620 passengers which Queen Mary 2 is capable of carrying across the Atlantic.

These two symbols of 21st century travel have much in common. They share a birthplace in St Nazaire where Airbuses are assembled and Queen Mary 2 was built. While QM2 reigns supreme at sea, the A380 Airbus will become the largest, most advanced and most efficient commercial aircraft when it takes to the skies in 2006.

The entente between ocean and air has not always been so cordiale. By the 1960s jet setters were deserting liners for airliners and on the Queen Elizabeth it was possible to be the only person at afternoon tea. The death of ocean travel was widely predicted.

What people forgot, however, was that *'Getting there is half the fun.'* Cunard came to terms with its rival by offering a joint crossing of the Atlantic, out by ocean and back by air. The entente was cemented in 1983 when for the first time QE2 partnered Concorde, the fastest and most luxurious commercial aircraft ever built, and Cunard soon became the largest charterer of the queen of the skies. Sadly Concorde carried her last passengers across the Atlantic less than three months before QM2 set out on her maiden voyage.

Above When the Queen Mary made her maiden voyage, the ultimate in luxurious land travel was the Pullman. 65 sleeper trains would be needed to carry her 2,075 passengers.

IMPERIAL OR THERMIDOR

Maine lobsters are to seafood as QM2 is to liners, both thriving in the ice cold waters of the North Atlantic. Passengers on QM2 consume 62,426lbs of lobster a year, the equivalent of the catch harvested by three Maine fishing boats constantly patrolling their pots.

If lobster is the world's ultimate white meat, caviar are its ultimate eggs. Caviar is the name given to the roe of the sturgeon, some of which swim through the cold Atlantic before going up river to spawn.

Although QM2 is the world's largest single consumer of caviar, it is not the most expensive ingredient in her larder, that honour belonging to saffron, the world's most precious spice. More than 75,000 flowers from a rare crocus that grows round the Mediterranean are hand picked and dried to produce one pound of saffron threads. QM2's chefs open two packets of saffron every day to perfume the rice that complements the lobster.

Salt cod and kippers were standard fare on Cunarders until the 1890s when refrigerators revolutionised menus and produced the ice for the oysters. On QM2 mahi mahi, one of the world's most beautiful fish, and sharks' fins, one of its most expensive delicacies, are on the bill of fare.

Above 84 boxes of haddock, 12 barrels of red herring and 20 kegs of oysters were included in the regular fish order for the passengers and crew of the Lusitania.

STARGAZING

Mariners have always looked to the stars to guide their ships to port. Lovers have gazed up at them as the prelude to a kiss on the deserted deck of an Atlantic liner. Queen Mary 2 captures the knowledge and wonder of the starry heavens in the world's first planetarium at sea.

On early Cunarders passengers were expected to entertain themselves, passing the long hours by playing the deck games like quoits and tennis that are still played on QM2 today. As passenger comfort took precedence over delivering the Royal Mail, Cunard introduced many firsts at sea - the first piano, the first gymnasium, the first indoor swimming pool, the first library and the first children's playroom.

QM2 continues to set trends from the first planetarium at sea to the ocean's first al fresco cinema. She has the largest ballroom, library and lifelong learning centre afloat. While fashions in entertainment come and go, the romance of the great liners remains constant like the constellations, as new generations of Atlantic passengers experience the sun setting over the New York skyline or gaze up to Orion hunting in the night sky.

Above 'The latest screen productions will be shown in all classes.' Until the end of the Second World War when a dedicated facility was installed, the Queen Mary's main lounge doubled up as a cinema.

CHAMPAGNE, CHARDONNAY AND CLARET

Queen Mary 2 pops nearly a quarter of a million corks a year, which, if lined up, would scale the 29,035 feet heights of Mount Everest, the world's highest peak.

QM2 also pulls over 60,000 pints a year and brews its own beer at sea. In capturing the conviviality of an English pub, the Golden Lion continues the tradition set in 1911 by the Laconia whose smoking room was modelled on a real English inn complete with leaded windows and original fireplace.

One bar which most passengers will not visit is the Pig 'n' Whistle as, since the days of the Queen Mary, this is the area where the crew escape to relax. On the Queen Mary, world famous entertainers would slip away from the limelight to play or sing for the crew. Jazz maestro Duke Ellington may have tinkled the ivories of the Pig 'n' Whistle's battered old piano which, when the paint layers were scraped away, was discovered to be an 1840s concert grand. Champagne is the drink that conjures up the glory days of a Cunard crossing: passengers on QE2 have even been known to shave in its bubbles. Every day on the new Queen, over 1,000 bottles are fetched from the world's largest floating wine cellar.

Above Britain still ruled her Empire when the Queen Mary was launched in 1934 and Queen Mary, the wife of George V smashed a bottle of Australian wine rather than the traditional French champagne over her bows.

SAILING ON A MOON BEAM

Over her 40 year lifetime Queen Mary 2 will travel the equivalent of twelve times to the moon and back.

In her first few months alone, she will have made her maiden crossing of the Atlantic, dipped a toe in the Caribbean, called in at Rio for Carnival and watched the fireworks burst over the Statue of Liberty on US Independence Day. She will have been a hostess at the Olympic Games in Athens and will have proved her mettle during seven Atlantic crossings.

QE2 is the first and as yet the only ship to have travelled over five million nautical miles. She will make her final transatlantic crossing in tandem with a new Queen who in her lifetime will mark the centenary of Queens on the ocean. What journeys, what history, what adventures are in store for QM2? Will she be the last ever Atlantic liner or the first of a new breed?

As she journeys a seventh of the way to Mars in her lifetime will she witness the first step for mankind on a new planet?

Above If it were possible to sail round the Equator, it would take the Queen Mary a mere 26 days to make the voyage.

QUEEN MARY 2 PROFILE

Length	1132 feet (345 metres)
Height	237 feet (72 metres)
Width	135 feet (41 metres)
Gross tonnage	150,000 tons
Builder	ALSTOM Chantiers de l'Atlantique
Construction	Steel
Horsepower	157,000 hp
Engines	Four diesel engines and two gas turbines
Propulsion	Four pods each of 21.5 megawatts
Maximum speed	Over 30 knots
Owner	Cunard Line
Cost	£550m ($800m)
Passenger capacity	2,620
Crew	1,250
Port of registry	Southampton
Maiden voyage	12th January, 2004

Left An early sketch of the 'Skyline' concept.

A 164 YEAR OLD TRADITION

1840   Samuel Cunard's first ship, the Britannia, sets out on her maiden voyage.

1907   The first Book of Comparisons is published for the maiden voyages of the Mauretania and the Lusitania.

1936   The first Cunard Queen's maiden voyage is similarly honoured with 'The Queen Mary Book of Comparisons'.

1940   The Queen Elizabeth races across the Atlantic shrouded in wartime grey. Her official maiden voyage is not celebrated until 1947.

1967   Her Majesty Queen Elizabeth II launches QE2 two days before the Queen Mary makes her final Atlantic crossing.

2000   Cunard Line signs the contract for a new Atlantic liner, the first in nearly forty years.

2002   The keel of QM2 is laid in St Nazaire, France.

2003   QM2 takes to the sea for the first time as she is floated out of her dry dock.

2004   QM2 sets out on her maiden voyage from Southampton.

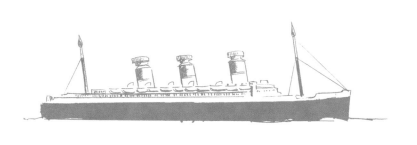